THIS BOOK BELONGS TO

____

I0380747

Have questions? We want to hear from you!
Email us at: support@activitywizo.com

Please consider writing a review!
Just visit: activitywizo.com/review

FREE BONUS

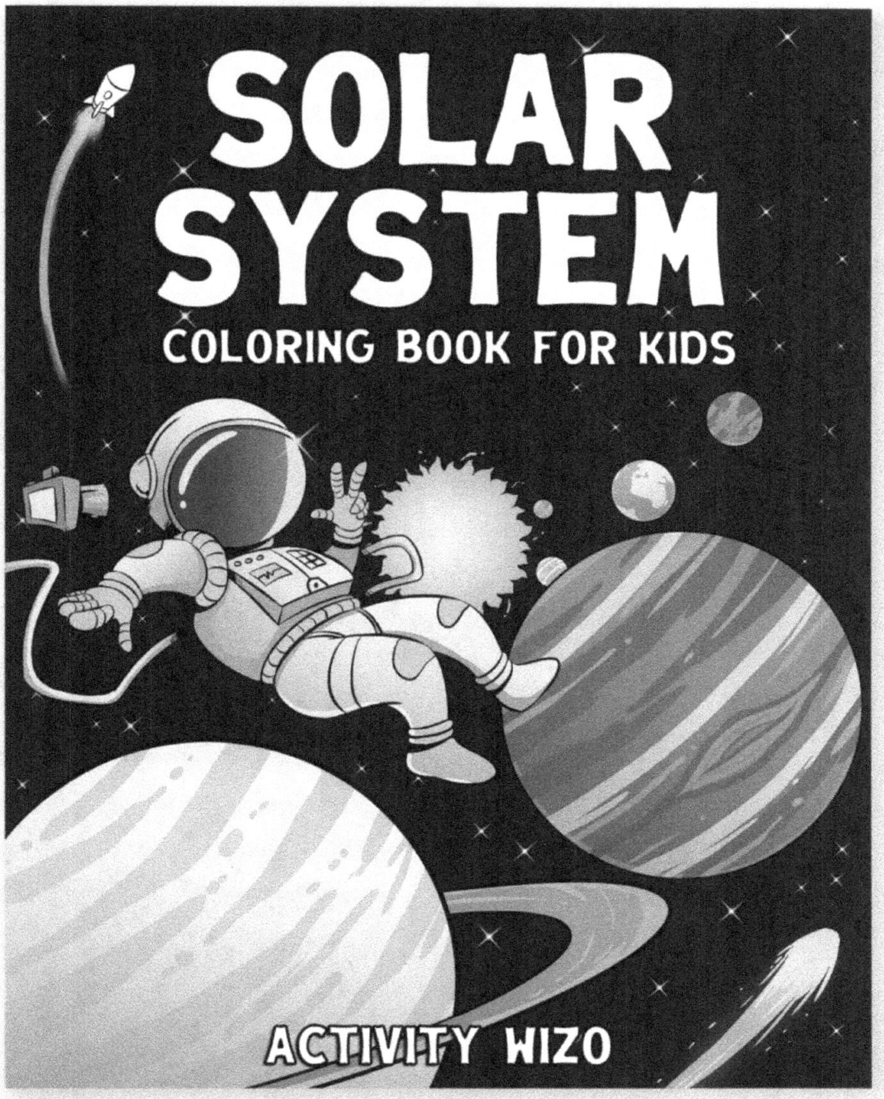

Just flip to the end of the book to get the link!

HAPPY
EASTER
TOO!

HAPPY
EASTER

FREE BONUS

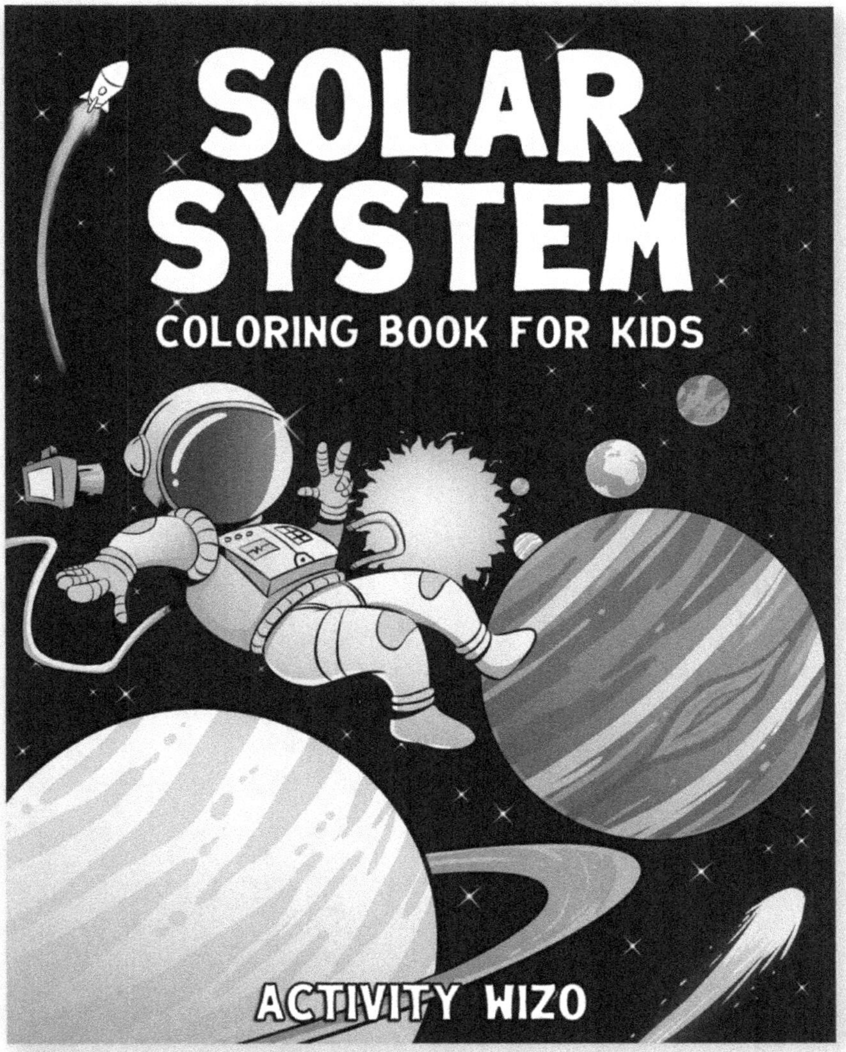

Get This FREE Bonus Now!

Just go to: activitywizo.com/free

www.ingramcontent.com/pod-product-compliance
Lightning Source LLC
Chambersburg PA
CBHW081756100526
44592CB00015B/2454
* 9 7 8 1 9 5 1 8 0 6 0 7 1 *